Journal

PETER PAUPER PRESS, INC.
WHITE PLAINS, NEW YORK

PETER PAUPER PRESS
Fine Books and Gifts Since 1928

OUR COMPANY

In 1928, at the age of twenty-two, Peter Beilenson began printing books on a small press in the basement of his parents' home in Larchmont, New York. Peter—and later, his wife, Edna—sought to create fine books that sold at "prices even a pauper could afford."

Today, still family owned and operated, Peter Pauper Press continues to honor our founders' legacy—and our customers' expectations—of beauty, quality, and value.

———

Cover illustration by Robert Vermet

Copyright © 2020
Peter Pauper Press, Inc.
202 Mamaroneck Avenue
White Plains, NY 10601 USA
All rights reserved
ISBN 978-1-4413-3229-5
Printed in Hong Kong
7 6 5 4 3 2 1

Visit us at www.peterpauper.com

MOOD TRACKER →

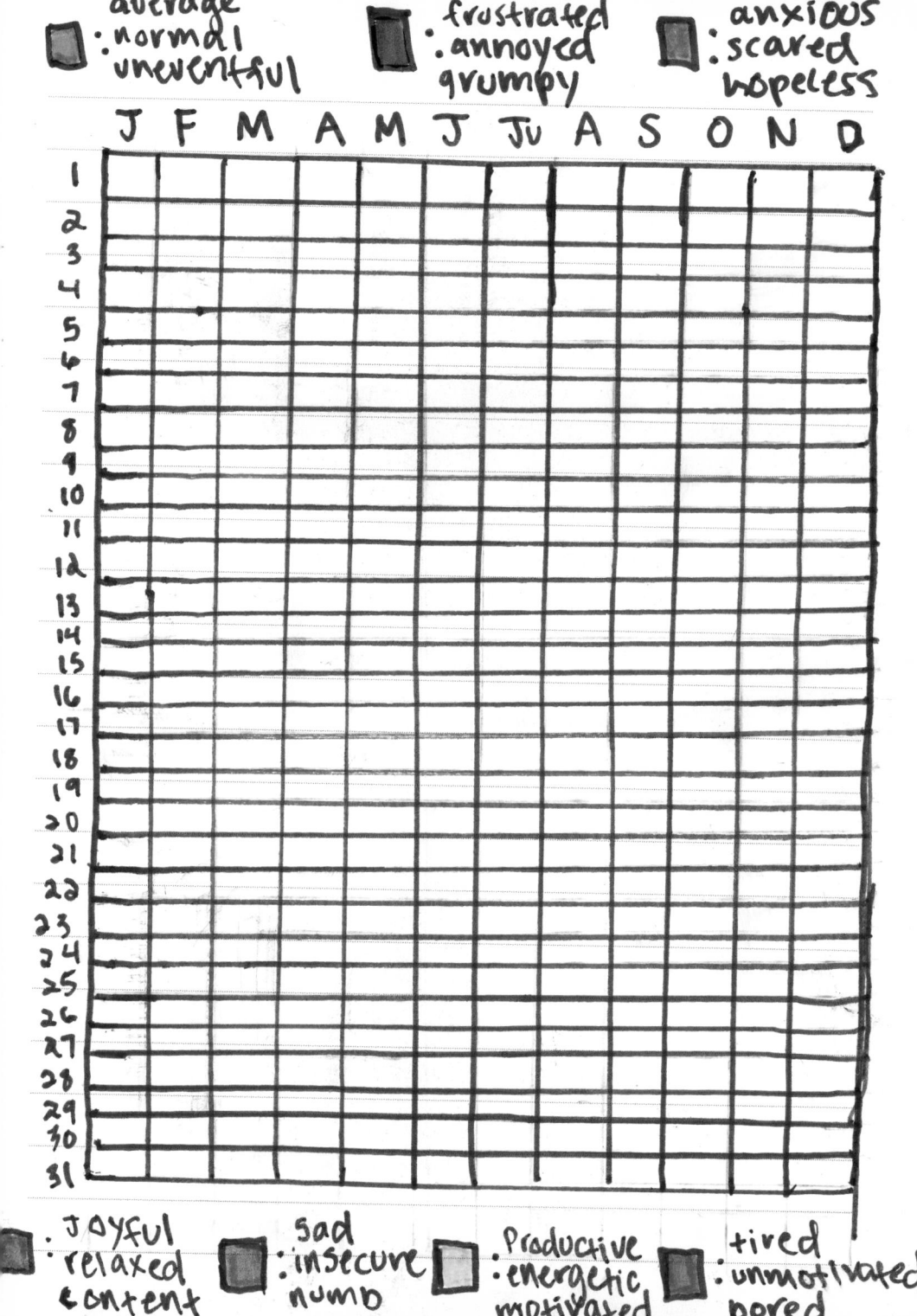

average
: normal
uneventful

frustrated
: annoyed
grumpy

anxious
: scared
hopeless

	J	F	M	A	M	J	Ju	A	S	O	N	D
1												
2												
3												
4												
5												
6												
7												
8												
9												
10												
11												
12												
13												
14												
15												
16												
17												
18												
19												
20												
21												
22												
23												
24												
25												
26												
27												
28												
29												
30												
31												

: Joyful
relaxed
content

sad
: insecure
numb

: Productive
energetic
motivated

tired
: unmotivated
bored

NEW TIRES

AMOUNT   DATE

GOAL:
$600

$600
$500
$400
$300
$200
$100

CREDIT CARD BILLS

PURCHASE	$$	PAID	CREDIT

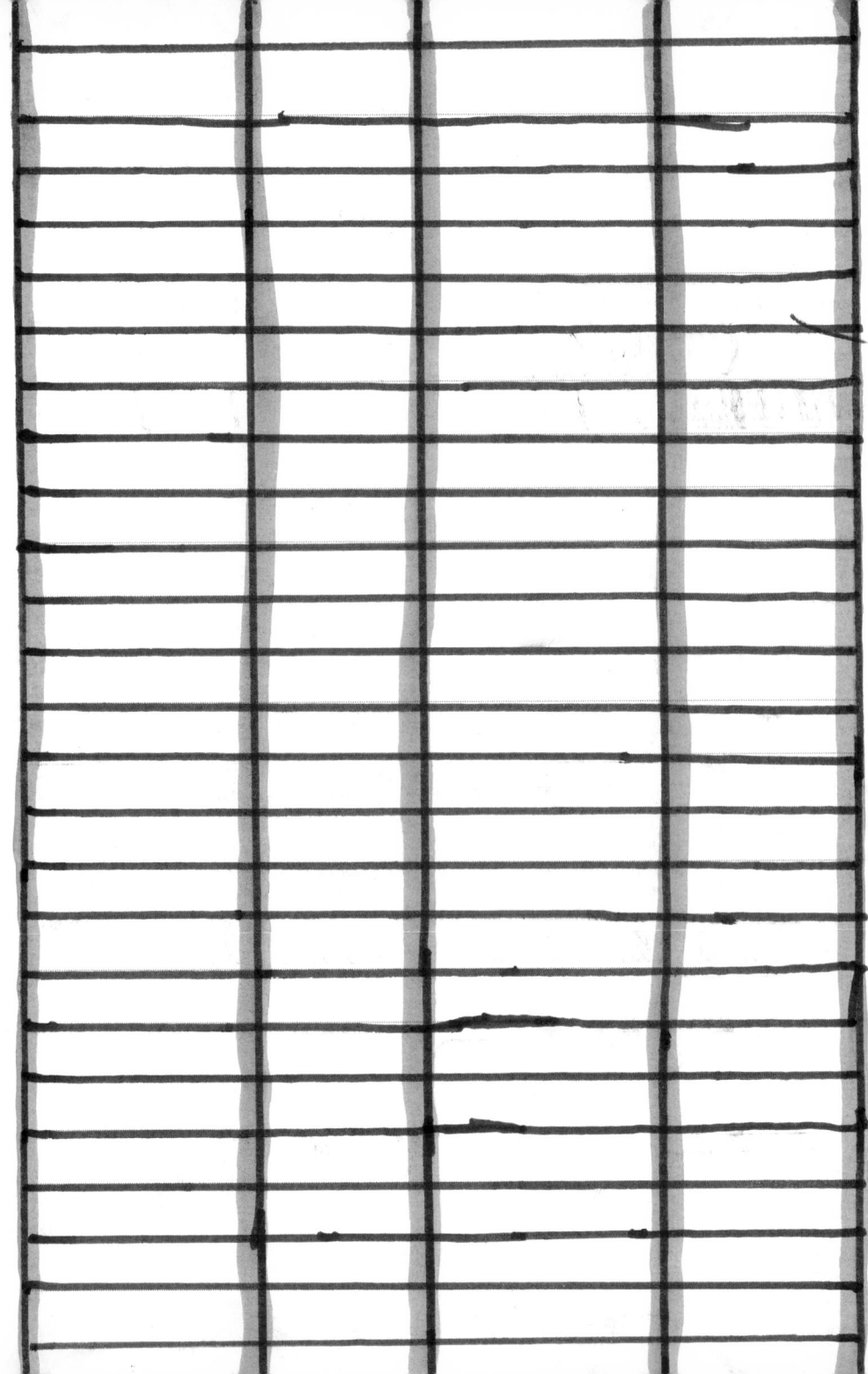

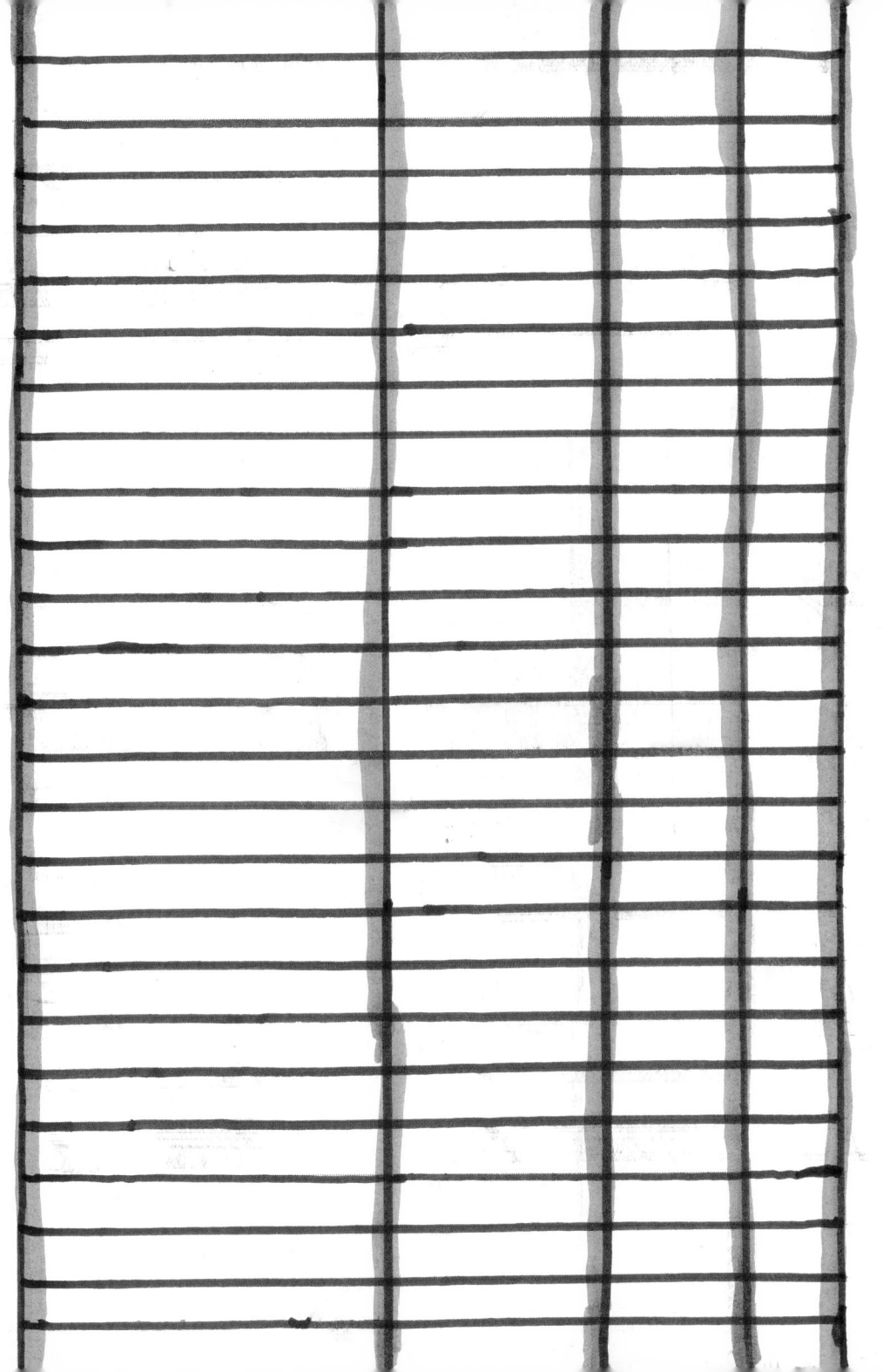

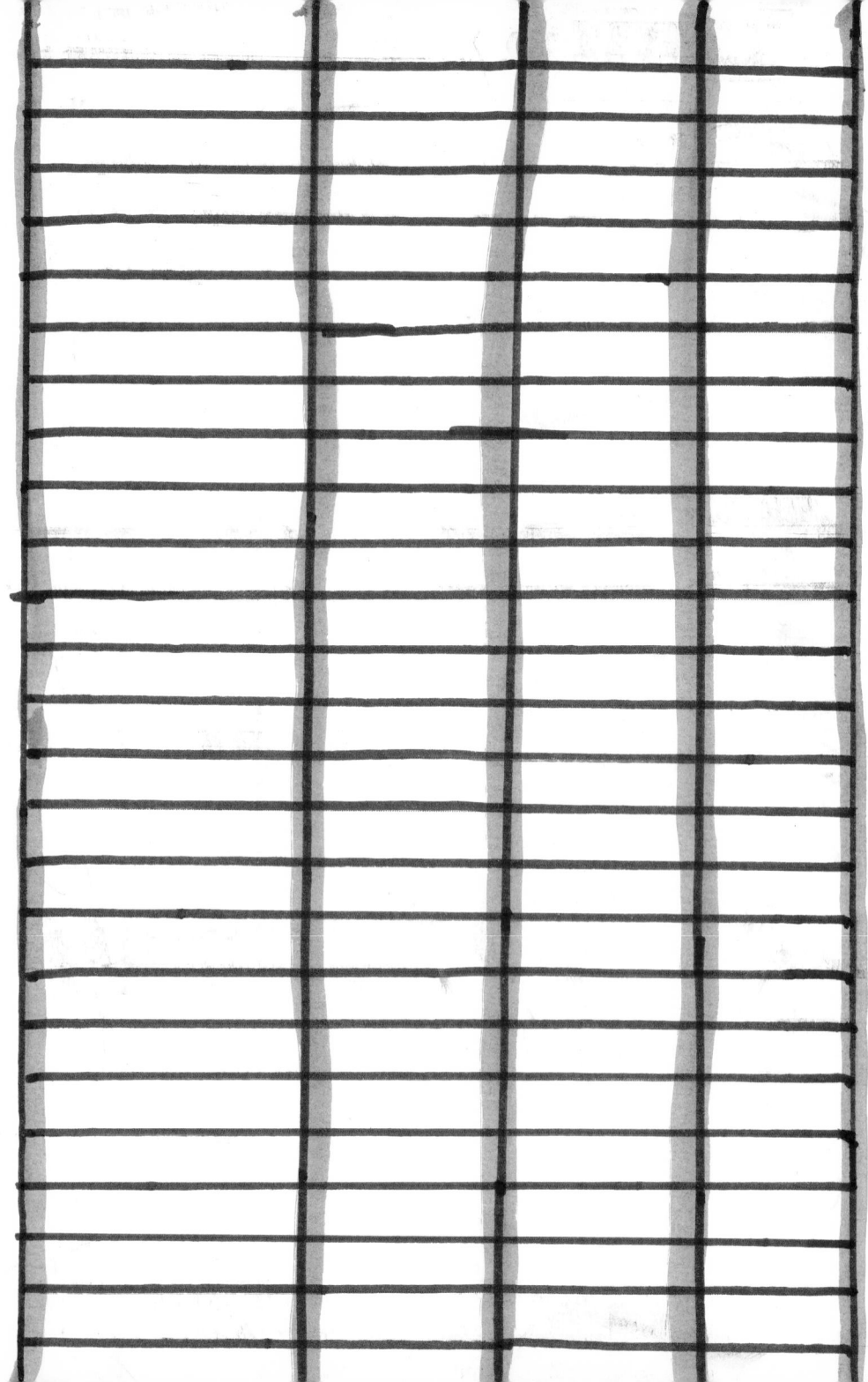

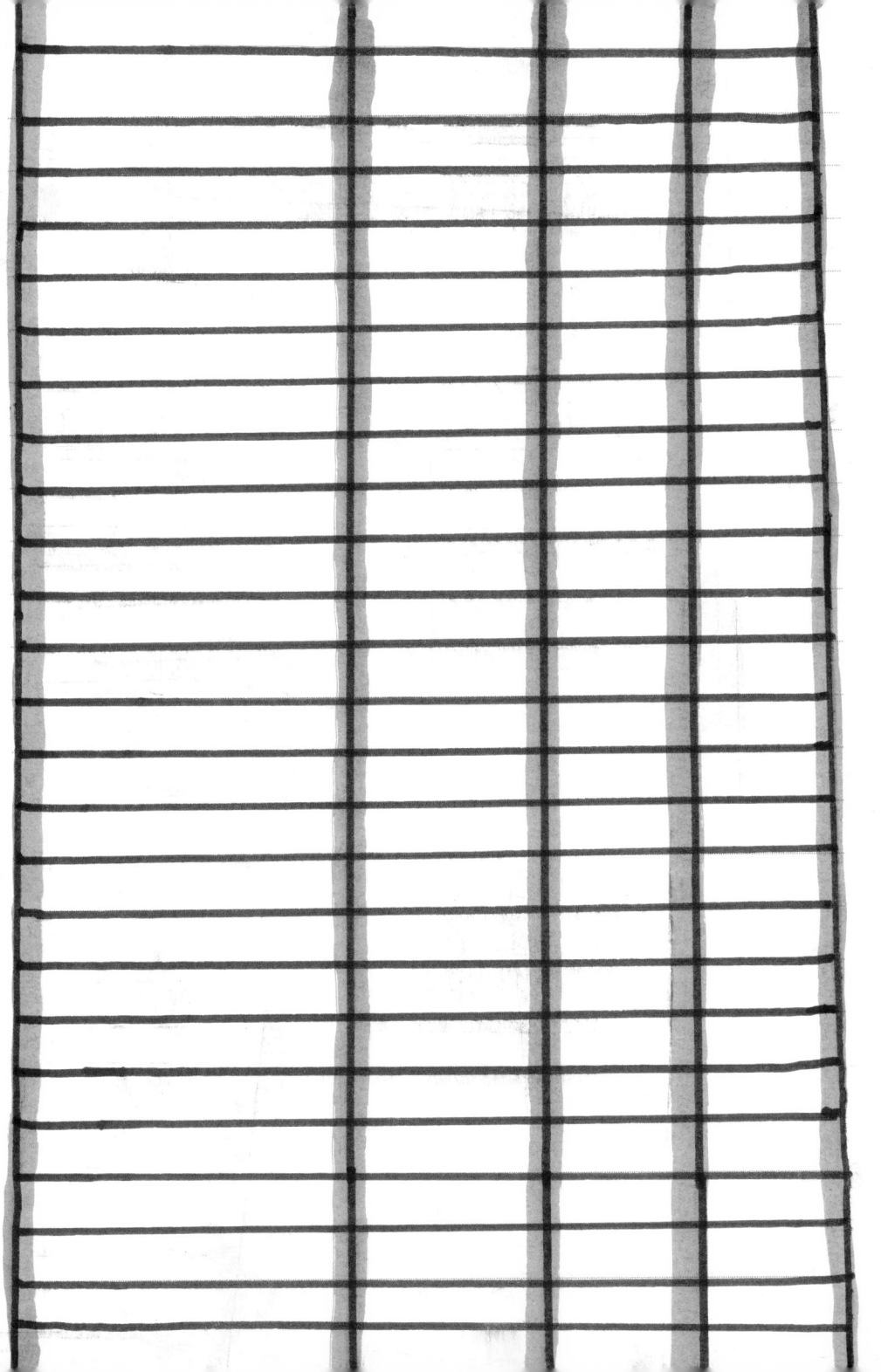

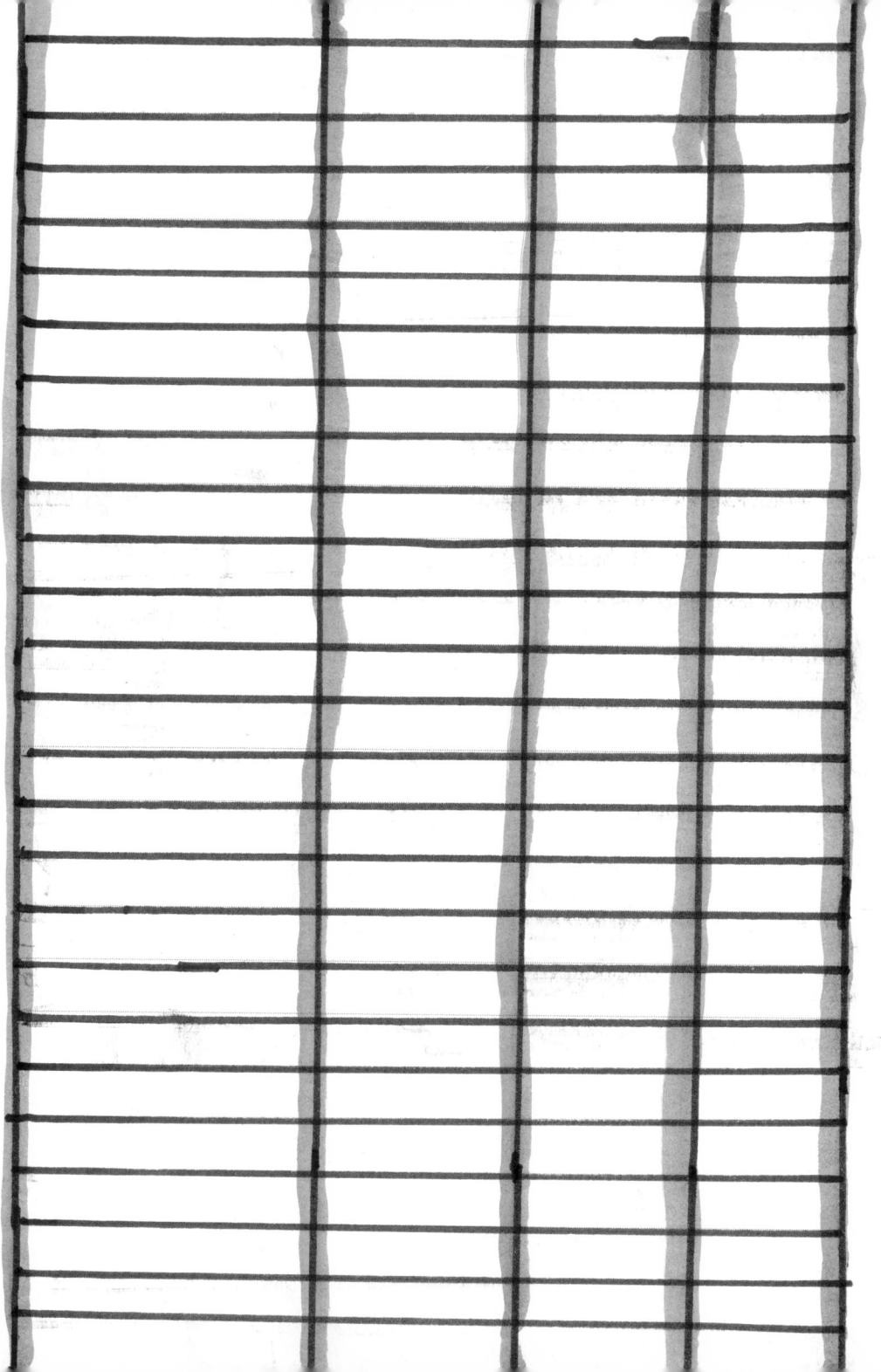

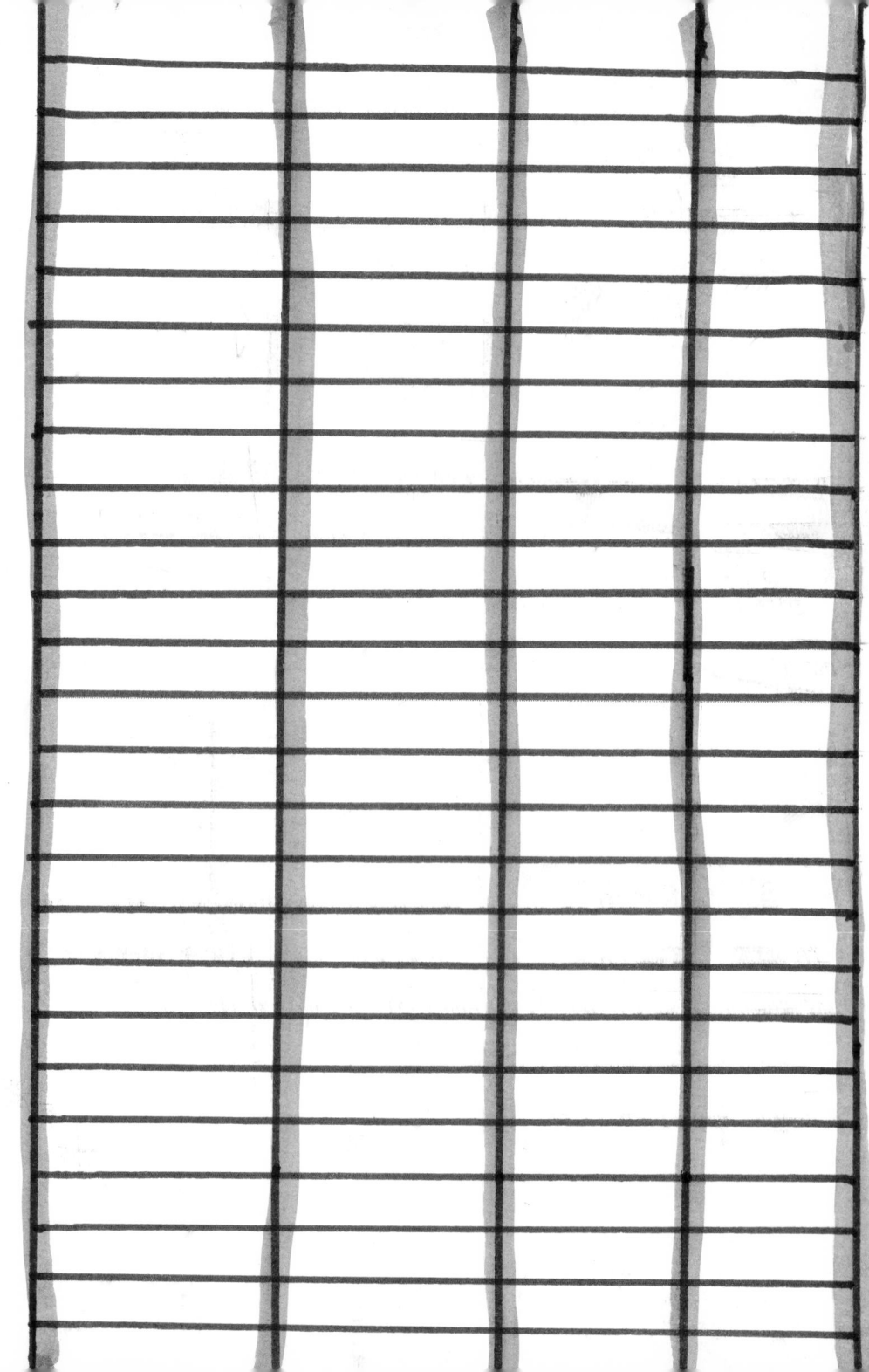

ACTIVITY IMPRESSION'S

ACTIVITY: WHY:	ACTIVITY: WHY:
ACTIVITY: WHY:	ACTIVITY: WHY:
ACTIVITY: WHY:	ACTIVITY: WHY:

Activity:	Activity:
Why:	Why:
Activity:	Activity:
Why:	Why:
Activity:	Activity:
Why:	Why:

Activity:	Activity:
why:	why:
Activity:	Activity:
why:	why:
Activity:	Activity:
why:	why:

Activity:

why:

Activity:

why:

Activity:

why:

Activity:

why:

Activity:

why:

Activity:

why:

Activity:	Activity:
why:	why:
Activity:	Activity:
why:	why:
Activity:	Activity:
why:	why:

Activity:	Activity:
Why:	Why:
Activity:	Activity:
Why:	Why:
Activity:	Activity:
Why:	Why:

Activity: Why:	Activity: Why:
Activity: Why:	Activity: Why:
Activity: Why:	Activity: Why:

Activity:	Activity:
Why:	Why:
Activity:	Activity:
Why:	Why:
Activity:	Activity:
Why:	Why:

Activity:	Activity:
why:	why:
Activity:	Activity:
why:	why:
Activity:	Activity:
why:	why:

Activity:	Activity:
why:	why:
Activity:	Activity:
why:	why:
Activity:	Activity:
why:	why:

Activity:	Activity:
Why:	Why:
Activity:	Activity:
Why:	Why:
Activity:	Activity:
Why:	Why:

Activity:

why:

Activity:

why:

Activity:

why:

Activity:

why:

Activity:

why:

Activity:

why:

Activity:	Activity:
why:	why:
Activity:	Activity:
why:	why:
Activity:	Activity:
why:	why:

Activity:	Activity:
why:	why:
Activity:	Activity:
why:	why:
Activity:	Activity:
why:	why.

Activity:	Activity:
why:	why:
Activity:	Activity:
why:	why:
Activity:	Activity:
why:	why:

Activity:	Activity:
why:	why:
Activity:	Activity:
why:	why:
Activity:	Activity:
why:	why:

Activity:	Activity:
why:	why:
Activity:	Activity:
why:	why:
Activity:	Activity:
why:	why:

Activity:	Activity:
why:	why:
Activity:	Activity:
why:	why:
Activity:	Activity:
why:	why:

Activity:	Activity:
why:	why:

Activity:	Activity:
why:	why:

Activity:	Activity:
why:	why:

Activity:	Activity:
why:	why:
Activity:	Activity:
why:	why:
Activity:	Activity:
why:	why:

Activity:	Activity:
Why:	Why:
Activity:	Activity:
Why:	Why:
Activity:	Activity:
Why:	Why:

Activity:	Activity:
Why:	Why:
Activity:	Activity:
Why:	Why:
Activity:	Activity:
Why:	Why:

Activity: why:	Activity: why:
Activity: why:	Activity: why:
Activity: why:	Activity: why:

Activity:	Activity:
Why:	Why:
Activity:	Activity:
Why:	Why:
Activity:	Activity:
Why:	Why:

Activity:

why:

Activity:

why:

Activity:

why:

Activity:

why:

Activity:

why:

Activity:

why:

Activity:	Activity:
why:	why:
Activity:	Activity:
why:	why:
Activity:	Activity:
why:	why:

Activity:

why:

Activity:

why:

Activity:

why:

Activity:

why:

Activity:

why:

Activity:

why:

Things To-Do @ work:
(when it's slow)

- journal
- meal plan
- bring a book to read
- research about neurotrasmitters
  - what each one does
  - dopamine, Serotonin, neureprinephen
  - what "sparks" or boosts each one
- list things that help ~~with~~ with my anxiety/depression
- list things that help my motivation
- list things that help with my happiness

Things To-DO @ work:
   (when it's slow)

-journal
-meal plan
~~dream~~
-research neurotransmitters
   · what the dic